D1171398

Appomattox Regional Library System
Hopewell, Virginia 23860
10/07

A Useful Dog

A Useful Dog

Donald McCaig

UNIVERSITY OF VIRGINIA PRESS
CHARLOTTESVILLE | LONDON

Grateful acknowledgment is made to
Bark, Outside, Long Island Newsday, and
All Things Considered, where some of these
essays first appeared, and to the Press on
Scroll Road, where a limited edition of
most of the essays was first published.

University of Virginia Press
Originally published in 2004 by Press on Scroll Road
© 2004 by Donald McCaig
"Uncle Harry" © 2007 by Donald McCaig
All rights reserved
Printed in the United States of America on acid-free paper

First University of Virginia Press edition published 2007

9 8 7 6 5 4 3 2 1

LIBRARY OF CONGRESS CATALOGING-IN-PUBLICATION DATA
McCaig, Donald.
   A useful dog / Donald McCaig. — 1st University of Virginia
Press ed.
      p.   cm.
   ISBN-13: 978-0-8139-2617-9 (cloth : alk. paper)
   1. Sheep dogs. 2. Sheep dog trials. I. Title.
   SF428.6.M33 2007
   636.737—dc22

                                        2006032913

Contents

A Useful Dog

A Sheepdog in Winter

THE SNOW is deep and he is old
but two hundred sheep are yarded
half a mile from feed so
I send him. The snow
is deeper than he is. He coils
himself below its
blank crust to buck into the light like a porpoise.
Each lunge, each crash back in flurry achieves,
    nearly,
three feet. He has eleven years
and must get eight hundred yards.
Too much love can burst the heart.

In trackless white he strikes
the black, trampled place the snowbacked sheep
have made and drops into his work.
I bid him be furious and dog bites
and dog pulls wool until the golden-eyed,
panting ewes are at my feet.

Sheep are forgetful creatures.
They make mud rushing from feeder
to identical feeder seeking perfection
of feed; something extra: they are like us.

Outside this dirty park, an exhausted sheepdog
nibbles the ice between his toes. I shade my eyes
against the glare. Whatever will I
do when he goes into the dark?
For half a mile his outrun is written
in snow: his track/his arc of fidelity
as bright, as fleeting as he is: as the snow.

Bringing the Lambs

EVERY MORNING, as soon as it's light enough to see without a flashlight, I go out with my sheepdog Gael to look for new lambs. It's frosty, and in the east the mountains are backlit red and there's a few stars and a three-quarters moon hangs over the western horizon. Sometimes a jet contrail streaks overhead, fat and pinkish in the sunrise: early travelers, thirty thousand feet over my head, reading the Washington Post, sipping their morning coffee.

Sheep are conservative creatures and most mornings we find them on the same hillside, strewn like groaning boulders. I tell Gael to wait while I slip in among them listening for the *uh-uh-uh* of a ewe talking to her new lamb. Sometimes I find a ewe having trouble but usually there'll be one, two, or three lambs tottering around Ma, trying to figure out which end has the milk on this, their first morning in the world. I scoop up the lambs and set off and most times Ma follows right behind, nickering anxiously. Gael checks out the birthplace hoping to locate a nice afterbirth for later consumption. Then she swings along behind the ewe.

Sometimes a ewe will panic and decide that the lambs dangling from my arms are not her idea of *real* lambs and she'll turn to run back to the birthplace, the last place she saw *real* lambs with their feet on the ground. It's Gael's job to keep her following me. Sometimes a first-time Mama will balk and refuse to follow so I set the lambs down and Gael and I shoo the new sheep family along, patiently, patiently, until we get near the barn and the sheep families already inside bleat their welcome.

Gael waits in the doorway while I sprinkle lime into a pen and bed it with fluffy straw. I close the gate on Mama and lambs and for the first time, I touch the ewe, grab her neck while I grope underneath and squirt a few squirts from each tit into the palm of my hand. I dip each lamb's navel in iodine, feed the ewe a leaf of our best alfalfa and a bucket of water. They always go for the water first. Birthing is thirsty work.

Sometimes Gael and I bring in one new mother, sometimes there's half a dozen and one day last week we fetched lambs from dawn until dark while my wife, Anne, eartagged and banded tails and gave medications. Dinner that night was a stew from the freezer and after dinner I laid down on the couch and stared at the NewsHour. Big doings in the big world. I do have opinions about those doings but for the life of me can't remember what they are. Gael is wiped out, curled up tight in her bed. Her front paws are twitching.

A Useful Dog

SCOTTISH SHEPHERDS say a dog is ready for a sheepdog trial when it has as many years as legs. They also say it takes ten years to make a sheepdog handler. I am not precocious. I've been trialing eleven years, and today, when I walk onto the trial field with Gael, canny spectators will grab their chance to visit the hamburger stand or line up for the Porta Potti. The entry fee for the Science Diet Blue Ridge Open Sheep Dog Trial was sixty dollars, and I won't see that money again. In previous years, with scores in the fifties and sixties out of one hundred, I've been lucky to get out of the basement; once I tied for dead last.

I am drinking coffee in Amanda Milliken's motor home on the second morning of the two-day trial. It is mid-May, the light is clear, dogwood is blooming. Faint whistles drift from the bowl-shaped trial field, where another dog is making its try. Amanda's dog Hazel is a black-and-white smooth-coated Border Collie. Hazel is musical and will sing along with *Oklahoma!* but her favorite tune is k. d. lang's song about the old coyote, especially the chorus, where she gets to howl.

That's enough, Hazel, Amanda says and the dog quits her musicale. *When do you run?* Amanda asks.

One, one thirty, I pull a face, get up and stretch. *Thanks for the coffee.*

The Blue Ridge Open is the first event in the Virginia Triple Crown, the most important trial series on the East Coast. The trial is what it says: open. Any dog, any age, any ownership, registered or unregistered, no papers required.

I don't suppose that half the trialists are farmers or ranchers. Nathan Mooney's a machinist, Jim

Lacy's a locksmith, Candace Terry works for a vet, and Sandy Dempewolf does something with NASA. At two years old, Stu Ligon's Chip is the youngest dog running. Bill Berhow's Jen is ten. The top three dogs from the previous year's National Finals—Tommy Wilson's Roy, Berhow's Jen, and Hubert Bailey's Rex—will compete against Gene Sheninger's four-year-old Meg, from Boonton, New Jersey, who is running her very first open trial.

When handlers aren't on the trial course themselves, they watch the other dogs. They set lawn chairs under awnings and critique each run. Sometimes the handlers know the dogs better than they know the people who own them. *That Pennsylvania fella with the June dog,* or *the woman with the dog out of Roy Johnson's Roscoe. That woman. Curly-headed.*

You can't buy a Border Collie puppy at the Blue Ridge Open; it's in the rules. Border Collies are animal athletes—powerful, brainy workaholics—and most pet owners can't handle one. After a few months of euphoria *(I've never seen a pup learn so fast)*, the dog grows up & soon afterward goes to the pound. Having a well-bred, full-grown Border Collie as a pet is like keeping Michael Milliken in your basement: *I'm going out to the store, Mikey. While I'm gone, please don't DO anything.*

Whoever wins today's trial will take home eight hundred dollars. Most of the sixty-two competitors won't win gas money. Lyle Boyer trials for the sheer complexity of it: *There's you, the dog, the sheep, the course, the weather, the time of day. . . . It's so hard to control all the variables to lay down a good run.*

In Yorkshire, we call it dogitis, says the English trial judge, Allan Heaton. *It's said to be incurable.*

A six-year-old, thirty-pound smooth-coat tricolor with prick ears, Gael is flirty, foxy, and hates to work in mud where she'll get her white paws dirty. But she'll stay with me through ice, rain, even mud, no matter how bitter—unless I raise my voice to her. Ladies, Gael believes, do not endure coarse language. Once, a few years ago, I completely lost it with Gael; I lifted my hand to smack her, and she said, *Oh dear.* I stuck my crude paw back in my pocket, where it belonged.

You canna abuse them. You canna, the shepherd who sold me Gael said. *They will never forget it was you that abused them.*

• • •

Gael enjoys the trials. She likes motels, but doesn't care for strangers fondling her (motel lobbies are awash in dog fondlers).

Although my young dog Harry wasn't entered, I brought him to accustom him to strange places, strange dogs, and hundreds of cars. Harry thought the trial's high point was last evening, after the last dog had run and the handlers turned out all their dogs to scombre and play. Harry had never seen so many dogs at once, racing over the grassy landscape. Given his druthers, Harry would be a social butterfly.

Sheep are brilliant at predator calculus—those that aren't don't survive to breed. Standing at the top of the trial course, the sheep evaluate the dog as it runs toward them: *Is it a sane dog? Responsible? Skilled? Can we beat it?* If you sent your family mutt raving out there, the sheep would blow full tilt through the nearest fence and keep running for miles. Sheep are not helpless.

Sheep trust Gael (that's good), but they lack respect for her (that's bad). With flighty sheep, Gael has an advantage; with stubborn sheep, she is too hesitant. She moves them, but too slowly and we run out of time.

These sheep are Barbados black bellies, which look more like goats than sheep: brown and black, high-headed hairy things. Common in the Caribbean, Barbs are parasite- and heat-tolerant and will endure more dogging than conventional sheep. Each sheep that comes onto the course today had run twice yesterday but since they're sorted randomly, no group is a stable flock. You might draw a ewe and three lambs, or four lambs, or two ewes and two lambs as I did yesterday (with the ewes quarreling over who was the leader). On the crossdrive, one of my ewes kept butting the other—wham, wham—and Gael grew slightly desperate. She glanced at me, *Donald, what shall I do with these distressing creatures?* I whistled her on, but we didn't get them into the pen. We got sixty-four points, another mediocre run.

The trial works like this. When you walk onto the course, you and your dog have nine minutes and one hundred points. Sitting in the horse trailer behind you, the judge subtracts points for every error. He can only subtract; he cannot add. Four sheep are set out on the top end of the course, 325 yards away. With a word, a whisper, or a prayer, you send your dog. The outrun to the sheep is instinctual; any Border Collie should be able to do it unaided, so each command you give means points off. The dog should make a wide swing behind the sheep, and approach without alarming them. The moment the two species make contact is the lift. The dog says, *Look at me. Do exactly as I say and nothing awful will happen to you.* If the sheep believe him, they start toward you. The dog then fetches the sheep straight to you, steers them around behind you, and drives them away 125 yards through a freestanding gate. Then across the field, perhaps two hundred yards, through the crossdrive gate, and directly to the pen. For the first time you can leave the post without disqualification. At the six-by-nine-foot box pen you pick up the six-foot rope attached to the gate. You and your dog then convince the sheep—against their better judgement—to walk into the pen. After closing the gate, you turn the sheep out again and hurry into a ring outlined in sawdust for the shed, where the dog splits two sheep from their mates and marches them away.

Each task must be executed elegantly and quietly. At the shed, for example, the judge will deduct one point each time a sheep steps out of the ring, four points for every failed attempt to split the sheep, three points for each missed opportunity. And, of course, the clock is ticking away.

If you retire, that's zero. If your dog chases the

sheep off course or freaks out, you are disqualified: zero. If your dog bites a sheep, DQ: zero. Although no two groups of sheep behave the same and sheep run better or worse during the course of a day the judge takes none of this into account. A shepherd cannot always choose his work.

The dog's commands are *away to me* (go around to the right), *come by* (around to the left), *this one* (shed this sheep), *stand, lie down, walk up* (toward your sheep), and *look back* (you've missed some sheep, leave the ones you have and go back out for the rest). Handlers can command by voice or whistle, but Gael prefers the whistle. Whistles are more precise than voices, and subtler at great distances. At half a mile, a shout is a shout.

The dogs' lives are too short. Bill Berhow's Nick was entered here but on the way Nick got sick so Bill left him at the vet school in Blacksburg. *Anything it takes,* Bill said, *whatever it costs.* Ralph Pulfer's Dan and Bruce Fogt's grand bitch Hope died last year. My Pip died last November 22. Pip loved this trial. He'd climb into the front seat and wag his tail as soon as we turned into these grounds.

On the course, Tommy Wilson's Ben has one sheep that won't go into the pen. The ewe walks in all right, but before her pals can follow, she panics, wheels, and bolts back out. Ben pushes, pushes, and the ewe goes in again & zap, she pivots and leaps, and Tommy tries to catch her in the air but misses. The judge calls, *Time,* and Tommy makes a rifle of his shepherd's crook and aims it at the victorious ewe and everyone laughs.

The announcer says, *Jim Chandler, Meridian, Mississippi, at the post. George Conboy on deck. Donald McCaig in the hole.* I am sick to my stomach. Why do I do this thing that makes me feel so bad?

• • •

At the car I say, *Not you, Harry; not this time,* and I walk Gael to the woven-wire fence that encloses the course so she can see the sheep at the top. She sees them, you bet. Trembles ripple from snout to tail. I walk her away so she can relieve herself if she wishes—which she doesn't. Gael never eats the morning of a trial, and neither do I. Food would be a lump in my stomach.

I walk onto the course into a new world. It is hushed; I can't hear the crowd or the announcer; I can't hear cars leaving or arriving. It's like one of those small rooms in a funeral parlor—the same pressure in my ears.

I am breathing fast and shallow, fearful that (a) Gael will come up short on her outrun (minus two) so I'd whistle her on (two more), or that (b) she'll lose confidence at the lift and the sheep won't move off for her (minus three to five), or that (c) they'll come on so slowly we won't be able to get them through the drive (minus fifty), or that (d) we won't finish the pen (minus twenty) or the shed (minus ten).

At my side, Gael is cocked, all aquiver. Her eyes say, *Trust me.*

I swallow. *Come by,* I say.

Gael shoots off, somewhat tight, and the slope of the course draws her in tighter. I put my whistle to my mouth but at the last minute she remembers where the sheep are and throws herself out and vanishes over the lip of the hill. I count one, two, and Gael is visible again along the ridgeline. Is she slowing? Will she stop? No, she is behind her sheep, and my first whistle command is *Walk up*. The sheep come off softly, on line for the gates but a bit heavy to the left, so I whistle Gael around to that side to keep them coming straight. It's a little like billiards, except the balls are alive.

I've drawn four yearling ewes; none wants to be leader. They tiptoe toward me and the spectators behind me.

Walk up, Gael, I whistle. *Walk up, walk up. WILL YOU WALK UP!*

When the sheep get around me and put the crowd behind them, they are delirious with relief, and fly away like bats, veering left, so I hurry Gael around to straighten them. Everything happens lickety-split. *Away, Gael,* I whistle. She whips right and turns them straight through the drive gates. *Awaay-to-meee!* She goes out wide to keep control, and then I am whistling, *Walk up, walk up,* and she pushes them smartly along the crossdrive.

As the sheep clamber up the slope toward the crossdrive gates, I have an out-of-body experience. I am not me, not the sheep, not the dog; I am the moving pressure-point, hundreds of yards out on that slope, exactly where Gael needs to be to get the sheep through those gates.

Away, I say, and she hooks right to frustrate an escape by a freethinking ewe.

They are through the gate now, and Gael is on their heels like a haunt and they turn nicely toward the pen.

Once I grab the gate rope I may not let go of it, but sheep don't know that. Penning sheep is a problem in the geometry of power. The sheep are more afraid of the pen than of me or Gael alone, but together we can pen them. The lead ewe swivels her head frantically, high-headed, on her toes, looking to bolt, and I give her all the room she needs to do what I want her to do. The sheep are bunched in the pen gate, the rear sheep pressing the front ones and the lead sheep eyes my rope, wondering, *Can I jump that?* I flick the rope so it becomes an ugly, snaky, sheep-hostile thing, and the ewe gives up and leads the other three into the pen.

Quick, I bang the gate shut.

Open the gate, the sheep take off down the hill, I jog into the shedding ring.

No idea how much time we have left—not much—but I must take a second to settle the sheep. Terrified sheep bunch up and you can't shed them. I want the four sheep lined up nose to tail so I can make a space between two couples and call Gael through. There, in that tiny space, Gael will pivot and take two away.

The damn sheep keep swirling, won't line up, and I see my chance but they break three/one instead of two/two, so I step back and ask Gael to regather them. She lines them up; again they break three/one. When I back up again, they split two/two of their own accord, but I am too slow to take advantage, and the judge calls, *Time.*

That's that. My ears are ringing, and my legs are wobbly. Gael hops into the cool-off tub at the edge of the course and laps the murky water.

Roy Johnson comes over, grinning. *Congratulations, partner. How do you feel?*

I say, *Gael's a pretty thing, isn't she?* I don't say I was sick to my stomach and afraid I'd cry.

Barbara Ligon says, *Do you know what you got, without the shed? Eighty-four points—without the shed!*

A friend shakes his head. *Too bad about that shed.*

I agreed, yes, yes, my best run ever; it is too bad.

Later, on the very last run of the day, Lyle Boyer and Jock earn a blazing ninety-seven points to win the trial. If Gael and I had gotten our shed, we'd have come third. As it is, we finish twentieth.

. . .

It is nearly three hours from the trial grounds to the farm, most of it by Interstate. Harry rides in back, Gael on the passenger floorboard nestled against the transmission hump. I haven't eaten anything all day, but I'm not particularly hungry. I'm not thinking, but I'm not not thinking, either.

Like most people, I am generally distracted, baffled by life. Most of the time, a microphone placed in my head would record: Does she love me? Where's the money coming from? I miss you, Pip. Call 800-966-4637 if this driver is operating in an unsafe manner . . .

But not today. *Thank you, Gael. For nine minutes, out on that trial field, you made me whole.*

Passports

IT IS HARD to kill a dog. We put it off and we delay and when we finally do it we ask ourselves afterwards if there wasn't something more we might have done. And of course there was. Whenever you have to kill an animal, there is always something more you might have done to keep him alive. But after years with livestock and dogs, there comes a signal, faint but unmistakable that says: it is time. Ignoring that signal is cowardly: you are less willing to face your loss than the dog is to face his death.

Moose and I never quite got together. He was a nervous sheepdog and I wasn't a good enough trainer to soothe him. Oh, he could do routine chores alright and had a good life here on the farm. In the hot summer months he spent hours swimming in the river.

Last fall Moose started limping and the vet found a lump under his front leg and maybe we could catch the cancer if we amputated. Three days after his amputation he hopped out to the corral to help with chores. Moose got around pretty good & even learned to lift his leg again but no, we hadn't got it all, and a couple months later his right eye went blind and he started to smell bad. So now he's in a place where the sheep don't spook him; he's much calmer and his new trainer knows better than I did how to handle a dog.

The evening before I killed him, the three-legged, one-eyed sheepdog went out to help me feed. He kept the ewes off the feeders. All through the night he vomited and in the morning vomited his butter-enclosed aspirin tab.

Moose died here, where twelve years ago he was born and he's buried in the graveyard on the hill where I hope to be buried someday. Moose's mother and father were already on the hill.

We carried him to his grave on his sheepskin bed and set his letter underneath. My wife, Anne, writes a letter for every one of our dogs and I have never asked her what she writes. She says it's a passport and I like to think of Moose coming to the last river he will ever cross and offering the boatman his letter. *Oh, yes, I was a very good dog.*

But it may be, it just may be—all our dogs waiting on the far side of the river that Anne and I must one day cross—those letters may not be dogs' passports. They may be ours.

Dogs and Us

Above our camp the peaks of Montana's Gravelly Range line the horizon like the teeth of a beartrap. In early October it is warm in the day, ten degrees at night, but there's snow on the eleven-thousand-foot peaks, and John Helle is anxious to trail his last bands of sheep through the Notch while it's still doable. Two weeks ago the rest of his sheep crossed the ten-thousand-foot pass on their journey home.

The predators that prey on John's sheep—black bears, grizzlies, mountain lions, coyotes, and reintroduced gray wolves—feel urgency too, for the hard weather is coming, and creatures without a thick layer of fat won't see spring. The herders report *coyotes very bad,* and John's brother Tom Helle shot two coyotes yesterday.

Day or night, racing to investigate threats, John's big white guard dogs warn predators off with sharp barks. To a sheepman, their incessant barking is comforting, and last night we fell asleep to the guard dog lullaby.

Twenty years ago, I bought Pip, my first sheepdog pup. What Pip taught me changed the direction of my life. Studying why dogs can affect men so profoundly has taken me to places few visit.

Assisted by two guard dogs and two sheepdogs, each of John's sheepherders tends twelve hundred ewes and lambs. Tedeo's band forded the Ruby River yesterday afternoon & at first light, started the steep climb toward the Notch. Victor's band is crossing behind us as we mount our horses.

John's sheepdogs, Dilly, Pirate, Spot, and Grizzly, are circling John's horse, raring to go. Tired guard dogs yawn hugely as they lope past.

Every spring and fall John Helle trails his sheep

between his summer pasture and the Home ranch. Marked with stone cairns to keep sheepmen on the route when snow or sleet is flying, this trail has been used for a hundred years. It winds through stunted forests, up steep scree slopes, and is impassable by jeep or all-terrain vehicle. Even cattle couldn't manage it. *Without the dogs,* John Helle says, *it would be impossible.*

. . .

The common ancestors of wolf, coyote, sheepdog, and guard dog alike emerged thirty-seven million years ago right here in North America. The earliest canid, Hesperocyon, was a long-tailed, fox-size, semi-arboreal carnivore with the distinctive shearing teeth (carnassials) our dogs have today. A scant twelve million years later some canids—the Leptocyons—had evolved masticating teeth too, adding seeds, nuts, and vegetation to their meat diet. But the dominant canids, the Borophagines, opted for a meatier diet and became large, powerful bone crushers. Open savannas favored larger ungulates (mammoths, bison), which are difficult prey for solitary carnivores, and some Borophagines became cooperative hunters.

When the earth's climate cooled, the large animals upon which the Borophagines depended died out, and two and one-half million years ago they followed their food sources into evolutionary oblivion.

For many years, scientists thought the wolf-like Borophagine Tomarctus was the ancestor of modern canines, but from fossil dentition evidence, paleontologist Richard Tedford, of the Museum of Natural History, thinks the more adaptable Leptocyon was the true ancestor of modern dogs, wolves, and foxes. He believes the less specialized Leptocyons had a decisive evolutionary advantage.

Glaciation and sea-level changes during the Pleistocene allowed wolves to migrate between the New World and the Old.

Modern man (perhaps only a single small band) managed to slip past the great Sahara barrier and out of Africa some 140,000 years ago. In the Near East for the first time, men met wolves.

· · ·

Sheepman and sheepdog, both descendants of that ancient evolutionary encounter, push a bleating flood of sheep up a Montana trail which gets steeper and rockier. John Helle's sheep dogs course back & forth behind the sheep, while somewhere far ahead Tedeo's dogs keep the leaders to the trail. John's dogs obey his whistles, voice and hand commands to go left, go right, stop, lie down, and go back for sheep they've overlooked.

On my Virginia farm, my sheepdogs aren't taught hand commands. Otherwise, this is familiar work—though more arduous than any single day's work my dogs are asked to do.

· · ·

Archaeological interest in nonhuman species is recent, and dog evidence may not have been cataloged or retained by earlier archaeologists. Emeritus canine archaeologist Stanley Olsen recalls begging his colleagues at Harvard's Peabody Museum to *Save the bones!*

The oldest undisputed archaeological evidence of a human/dog connection is dogs buried in human graves twelve to fourteen thousand years ago in present-day Israel.

Fifty years ago Konrad Lorenz proposed the popular story of dog domestication. A child finds a wolf cub.

> The soft, round, wooly bundle no doubt elicited
> in that small daughter of the early Stone Age
> the desire to cuddle it and carry it around interminably. . . . The father, of course, wants to drown
> it straightaway, but the little daughter, weeping,
> clasps her father's knee so that he stumbles and
> drops the pup, and when he stoops to pick it
> up it is already in the arms of the child, who is
> standing in the farthest corner dissolved in tears.
> Not even a Stone Age father could be so stoneyhearted so the pup is allowed to stay.

While wolf cubs certainly can be tamed by humans, as a domestication scenario taming is unconvincing. Tamed wolves do not instantly become domestic dogs. The desire of tamed adult wolves to cooperate with humans is weak, and they can be dangerous. I think it unlikely any Stone Age father would introduce a powerful, dangerous predator into his family circle. He would be crazy to do so.

. . .

Last year the Helle family fed three hundred bags of dog food to their twenty-eight dogs. That's four herders with four dogs each, plus John's four sheepdogs, which go with him everywhere, and there's Tom Helle's dogs, and their father Joe Helle's dog, and the retired dogs, Ginger and Spike. John says, *Old Ginger gets real upset. She knows when I've been working sheep with the other dogs. When I come home, she'll have hidden all the dog dishes.*

．　．　．

In 1995 the postdoctoral geneticist Carles Vilà was puzzled by his own calculations. He'd been comparing wolf & dog mitochondrial DNA. The date coyotes evolved from the wolf had been established from fossils, and comparing coyote MDNA with wolf MDNA had established a rate of canid mutation. By comparing dog MDNA with wolf MDNA Vilà hoped to date dog origins but the figures weren't coming out right. Archaeological evidence showed that dogs had evolved no more than twenty thousand years ago. But Vilà's genetic evidence kept showing a much older date. After a couple sleepless nights he brought his calculations to his advisor, evolutionary geneticist Robert Wayne.

Vilà and Wayne were stunned to learn that, on the genetic evidence, the dog became a dog between 60,000 and 125,000 years ago.

They weren't happy with their finding. Mutation in MDNA is erratic. What if the canid mutation rate had changed? If the dog's genetic clock had sped up, the dog might have evolved when the archaeologists said it had. Perhaps the historically recent enthusiasm for dog show breeding had increased the rate of dog mutations.

So Wayne studied the Cholo (Mexican hairless), a dog population so isolated its genetic clock could not have been influenced by dog show breeding. Cholo DNA produced the same date as the earlier samples. He next took DNA samples from mummified Inca dogs and Inuit dogs entombed in Alaska permafrost for ten thousand years. Early results from these studies support Vilà/Wayne's original dating. When archaeologists decry the absence of dog bones in sixty-thousand-year-old human sites, Wayne suggests that perhaps early dogs—protodogs—weren't morphologically distinct from wolves.

Robert Wayne's domestication story is less sentimental than Konrad Lorenz's. Wayne thinks wolves were attracted to the scraps in human midden & humans didn't drive them away because these midden wolves warned humans of other, deadlier predators. Over thousands of years some of these wolves/protodogs/dogs became useful guardians and hunters. Others were eaten.

Some scientists were struck by the evidence that modern man and wolves arrived in the Near East at approximately the same time. Cal Tech professor John Allman has speculated that humans and dogs may have coevolved; that perhaps we thin-skinned humans survived during the last ice age rather than more cold tolerant Neanderthals because we had dogs & Neanderthals did not.

Allman told me that the wolf/protodog/dog provided humans *a superior sense of smell, superior hearing, and superior vision at night.*

• • •

When humans began to farm and build settlements, dogs started resembling modern dogs. The ancient Egyptians bred seventy varieties as hunters, guard dogs, war dogs, pets, healing dogs, and dogs bred for sacrifice.

The prehistoric canids' ability to fill many ecological niches was inherited by the dog, which exhibits a greater morphological variety than any other mammal. The 2-pound Chihuahua and 180-pound Bull Mastiff are equally *Canis familiarus*. If we humans exhibited similar variety, some adults would weigh 20 pounds, others nearly a ton. Dog's uses have been as various as his shapes: *Canis familiarus* hunts bears, birds, deer, foxes, coyotes, rats, gazelles, and lions. He guards against predators—human and other. He herds sheep, cows, hogs, geese, turkeys, goats, and reindeer. He has pulled travois, sleds, carts, and in the First World War, Maxim machine guns. In some protein-poor Asian and Polynesian cultures (and at times in modern Europe), dogs have been eaten. Dog skins have become human garments. Seizure detection dogs predict epileptic seizures so the victim can reach safety before being incapacitated. Dogs sniff out drugs. The dog hears for humans and sees for humans; he has always smelled for humans. After careful training and several weeks on the outskirts of a minefield to learn what belongs in that place and what does not, dogs detect land mines.

 •   •   •

A faded red star surmounts a battered concrete pylon beside the Albanian border station. We're a few hundred yards above the morning fog and the scorched hillside where NATO planes had bombed Serb positions a year before. The partially cleared minefield looked like a survey crew had been laying stakes & string for an unusually precise, unusually complicated building project. Deminers call these mines toe tappers: five or six ounces of explosive, pressure detonator, plastic case. If you're lucky, they'll break your foot. If you're unlucky, they'll blow your foot off.

For the deminers it's just a job, and they pause at the tin coffee shack across from the border station for a cup of thick Turkish coffee and shot of slivowitz before they don flak jackets and the helmets with protective face shields and start up the ridge, walking inside a previously cleared safe zone perhaps ten feet wide. From either side of that zone, each man-dog demining team works a marked square.

Stipo Mijatovic᾽ and Kim have been partners for four years. Stipo Mijatovic᾽ is a big, tough Croatian; Kim is the smallest German shepherd bitch I've ever seen. As we speak, Stipo's hand strokes Kim continuously.

Kim is trained to search, stop and observe, sit, and wait for the next command. When Kim alerts on a mine, she promptly sits & looks back to Stipo, who is right behind her. Stipo takes Kim to safety before he crawls forward to locate and disarm the mine. Albania's previous paranoid government placed a zillion ready-made circular pillboxes throughout the country and the deminers drop their finds into a nearby pillbox and detonate the lot from time to time.

Were Kim to bypass a mine without alerting, consequences to Stipo could be serious. And though infrequent, accidents do happen. Last spring the dog Ellis was distracted by a stray dog, stepped out of his marked square, and detonated a mine. The deminers evacuated Ellis to Pristina, and dissatisfied with the care, they medevaced the dog to Sarajevo, where his foot was saved. Ellis is getting physical therapy to return him to his job. These dogs were bought in Holland, trained in the United States, shipped over here, and are worth twenty thousand dollars each.

Stipo doesn't work Kim in wind or rain or if Kim is out of sorts. After thirty minutes of intense searching Kim and Stipo take a break in the safe zone and play a little ball.

When I ask Stipo if he trusts Kim, Stipo says, simply, *She has never failed to alert.*

When I ask Stipo what Kim thinks of him, the deminer stares at me incredulously before giving Kim's leash to a friend, who walks away with her. For a few yards Kim trots along calmly until she realizes she's being separated from the man who accompanies her into deadly peril every day of her life. Kim spins and lunges against the leash until she is back at Stipo's side, where Stipo resumes his incessant stroking. Kim looks up, as if to ask Stipo: *What on Earth did you do a crazy thing like that for?*

• • •

The most recent phase of dog evolution began in the nineteenth century. In 1866 Charles Dickens described how early dog shows were judged:

> The beauty of one dog, the ugliness of another, and of all the utmost development of the individual peculiarities of the species to which they belonged, would seem to be the causes operating with the judges. Prizes are to be won by size, by depth of chest, by clean finish of limb, and symmetry of points as in the case of the setter, the retriever, the greyhound, the pointer. Meanwhile to be bandy, blear-eyed, pink-nosed, blotchy, underhung, and utterly disreputable is the bulldog's proudest boast. The bloodhound's skin should hang in ghastly folds about his throat and jaws with a dewlap like a bull. The King Charles span-

iel wears a fringe upon his legs like a sailor's trousers, and has a nose turned up so abruptly that you could hang your hat upon it if it were not so desperately short. . . . Truly the qualifications of dogs are numerous, and very various their claims on our admiration.

Early dog shows were part pet show, part business, part curiosity; one enterprising American dentist exhibited a dog whose teeth he'd replaced with gold inlays. Crowded dog shows were terribly unhealthy for dogs and promoters lost money on them. Cheating was so prevalent that the Kennel Club in the United Kingdom and later the American Kennel Club (AKC) were organized to regulate the shows.

People soon began to think that purebred dogs registered by the kennel clubs were rather special. As one commentator put it: *I hope and trust that the time is not very far distant when either ladies or gentlemen will be ashamed to walk in the street in the somewhat vulgar company of mongrels.*

The English dog food salesman Charles Cruft may never have owned a dog himself (his wife said not), but Cruft was a brilliant promoter who knew how to bring in crowds and run a profitable dog show. One hundred eight years after Charles Cruft organized it, Crufts is the biggest dog show in the world. The Kennel Club has run Crufts since 1948 & won't say how much money it makes.

In four days Crufts attracts 150,000 visitors. There are SAR (search and rescue) dogs, dog training demonstrations, agility and obedience competitions. Here a sheepdog is herding ducks; there's the agility team made up entirely of shelter dogs—big and little dogs, mutts & purebreds. How the crowd cheers when the twelve-year-old greyhound clambers up, up, and over the steep incline!

By noon of the second day my feet hurt. You can buy postcards, souvenir mugs, original paintings of your dog. Doghouses, dog crates, and dog trailers are available. Dog food companies offer free samples and hospitality booths where the footsore spectator can sit and drink a cup of tea. I visited four booksellers specializing in antiquarian dog books.

And there are twenty-six thousand dogs at Crufts, all the dogs anyone could ever want to see. At the breed club booths you can get information and greet dogs that somehow put up with a zillion visitors, all those kids who want to pet or tickle or rub them on the belly.

But Crufts' main event is the dog show. First all the breeds are judged, then the Best in one Breed is judged against winners of similar breeds to become a Group Winner. On the final evening of the show, in the center ring, the Kerry Blue Terrier and the other Group Winners (a Bearded Collie, a Toy Poodle, a Saluki, a Bichon Frise, a Boxer, and a Cocker Spaniel) stood for the judge's inspection, trotted briskly around the ring, turned this way and that until the judge awarded Best in Show to Kelly Blue Terrier Ch. Torums Scarf Michael. Truly the qualifications of dogs are numerous, and very various their claims on our admiration.

Dog shows standardized breed morphologies and preserved breeds that otherwise might have gone extinct, like the bulldog, originally bred for bullfighting, and the Dalmatian, originally a coachman's dog. But there was a price. Many show dogs have evolved into highly stylized, exaggerated beasts that don't look like or work like their ancestors. Herding dogs that can't herd, hunting dogs that can't hunt, and water dogs that can't swim well are commonplace.

Unfortunately for purebred dogs, genetic diseases became commonplace too.

• • •

I haven't asked sheepman John Helle if his dogs are registered with any kennel club; I assume not. Most of his sheepdogs are Border Collies, one aged Australian shepherd pants by me on the trail. John's guard dogs are big white fluffy dogs I can't tell apart: Maremmas, Anatolian shepherds, and the Akbash Muggsy, who is in the dog house. After John's first sheep left summer pasture, Muggsy decided to walk seventy miles home too. Enroute he paused to check out Shaggy's flock, and the two got into a fight. Afterward the two dogs made up and decided to trail out with John's brother's band. *It's hard to keep the guard dogs in place,* John says, *when the sheep are moving around.*

• • •

In that 1866 report Dickens contrasted the fashionable dog show with a decidedly unfashionable show:

> As soon as you come within sight . . . some twenty or thirty dogs of every conceivable and inconceivable breed, rush towards the bars, and, flattening their poor snouts against the wires, ask in their own peculiar and forcible language whether you are their master come at last to claim them?
>
> For this second dog show is nothing more nor less than the show of the Lost Dogs of the metropolis—the poor vagrant homeless curs that one sees looking out for a dinner in the gutter, or

curled up in a doorway taking refuge from their troubles in sleep. To rescue these miserable animals from slow starvation, to provide an asylum where, if it is of the slightest use, they can be restored with food, and kept till a situation can be found for them; or where the utterly useless and diseased cur can be in an instant put out of his misery . . . to effect these objects, and also to provide a means of restoring lost dogs to their owners, a society has actually been formed.

That society, that unfashionable dog show, persists today as London's Battersea Dog's Home. Although Battersea is justifiably proud of its spanking new state-of-the-art facility (it has ramps instead of stairs because dogs don't like stairs), some original Victorian kennels are still in use.

A handsome young Rottweiler had been abandoned outside the Dog's Home. In its expensive crate the dog was drooling, urinating and whining in fear. The security guard who brought the dog inside had tattoos, body piercings, and very gentle eyes.

Security? I asked.

Oh yeah, he said. *Sometimes people come drunk. Sometimes they drop a dog and come back a couple hours later and want it back.*

Battersea takes in dogs 24 hours a day, 365 days a year, and rehomes almost all of them. Groomers, trainers, and vets make the dogs presentable, amenable, and healthy. (Later that morning I saw that terrified Rottweiler a second time: cleaned up, vet checked, and trotting contentedly behind a Battersea staffer.) Four Battersea vans visit London's police stations, collecting the city's strays.

Dog's Home staffers interview prospective owners to make a proper match and make home visits to ensure the match will last for a lifetime.

• • •

In September the Dog's Home holds its annual reunion, and last year three thousand rehomed dogs & seven thousand people came to nearby Battersea Park to try their dogs in races and agility games, costume them as Queen Elizabeth the First or Sherlock Holmes or something equally, wonderfully ridiculous. (I particularly admired Gus, the tiny Papillon done up as a bee.) People come from all over Britain just to spend a pleasant fall day with others as dotty as they are about their dogs.

Since I am certifiably dog dotty and had been away from my own dogs for too long, I was dog bereft and arrived too early, while the staff was still setting up the tents. The only dog in sight was a huge, beautiful German shepherd and I struck up a conversation with the dog's young owner.

Lucas, the beautiful shepherd, was just ten months old but severely dysplastic. Dysplasia (the dog's femur can't stay in its pelvic socket) is genetic and not uncommon in big German shepherds.

He'll get his second x-rays next week, the young man said. The young man wasn't dressed like someone who could easily afford diagnostic x-rays.

Lucas can't play with other dogs. If he starts running and jumping, he's in awful pain. It breaks my heart, really. He'd so like to play with the others.

Well, I say stupidly, *I hope you enjoy the day.*

Oh, we can't stay. It'd get him too excited like. I just thought I'd bring him over early, before the other dogs came, so Lucas could be part of the reunion. After a pause he added, *They say he won't live to be more than six.* He touched Lucas' beautiful head, softly. *Still . . .*

• • •

At ten thousand feet the sheep trail crosses steep, unstable scree, and I scramble along, leading my horse. A couple years ago a sheep got lost up here, and next day, when John Helle returned for it, the sheep was trying to join a band of mountain goats. I asked John if the trail wasn't dangerous in bad weather, and he said he'd lost a couple of packhorses but never a dog or human.

The Notch is a broad alpine meadow between Stonehouse and Springcrest Mountains, and the sheep snatch grass as they hurry across. Dilly pauses to roll and rub herself in a patch of snow. One of the guard dogs ambles past.

I can't see a house or road or electric line. The distant mountains, the Teton range, are insubstantial as ghosts, two hundred miles away. Long-dead sheepherders built a stone cairn on the Notch & made the faint sheep trails that traverse the sheer mountainsides.

On my farm back in Virginia, I've six sheepdogs and a guard dog. One day I will be buried on the hill where my dogs Pip and Silk and Mack and Gael are buried. I eat lunch while John and his dogs go back to hurry Victor's band along.

• • •

Every known genetic disease can be found in mongrel dogs but occurrences of any one disease are rare. Studies show that mongrels live longer and are healthier than registered purebred dogs.

Believing they could breed for the good and cull the bad, dog show breeders bred closely related dogs from closed, sometimes tiny populations (the foundation stock of some breeds is fewer than a dozen animals). What purebred breeders unwittingly did by closing registries and inbreeding concentrated genetic diseases. Dwarfism, blindness, deafness, lameness, aggression, bleeding, autoimmune disorders, and early death are caused by the four to five hundred different genetic diseases found in purebred dogs.

Over time, the cumulative effect of purebred breeders' practices began to be felt by ordinary pet owners, many of whom trusted that kennel club registration and a championship or two in the dog's pedigree ensured a superior dog that would be, if nothing else, healthy. In *Time* magazine's November 1994 cover story, "The Shame of Overbreeding," the magazine estimated that one in four purebred dogs was afflicted by genetic disease. Not long afterward the American Kennel Club established its Canine Health Foundation.

· · ·

In 1991 Jasper Rine, director of the Human Genome project at Lawrence Berkeley National Laboratory, and his associate, Elaine Ostrander, began mapping the dog genome. Since 90 percent of human DNA is identical to dog DNA and 60 percent of dog genetic diseases correspond to human diseases, geneticists hoped that locating the gene for a dog disease would make it easier to locate its human counterpart. Rine and Ostrander also thought the genetic map would help locate dog genetic diseases.

The AKC's Canine Health Foundation has been a major funder of dog genome mapping and has funded research into specific diseases as well. This year it will spend more than a million dollars.

Though the dog genome map is incomplete, two-thirds of the dog's chromosomes have been identified, and two dozen dog diseases have already been located, including genes for the bleeding disorder Von Willibrand's disease and the progressive retinal atrophy that blinded Irish Setters. Those who hoped dog genome information would provide clues to human ailments were vindicated when finding the gene that causes narcolepsy in Doberman Pinschers helped locate the human narcolepsy gene.

Cornell geneticist Gregory Acland estimates that most single-gene dog diseases will be located within the next twenty years.

And as Deborah Lynch, Director of the Canine Health Foundation, told me, purebred dog breeders who once whispered about genetic problems (if they talked about them at all) have embraced this new research enthusiastically. Indeed, some breed clubs have hired scientists to determine which genetic diseases most afflict their breed. Lynch told me, *It's almost like coming out of the darkness into the light.*

• • •

Climbing down from the Notch is no easier than climbing up, and we lead the horses. At the head of his twelve hundred sheep Tedeo can't see or command his dogs bringing up the rear, so the dogs must work on their own. Tedeo trusts his dogs to keep the sheep moving, to bring every single sheep, to find and fetch that errant ewe and her lamb that have refuged in an alder thicket.

The dogs pause for a drink at a spring in a glade some early romantic settler named Honeymoon Park.

· · ·

Identifying the mutant gene(s) that causes a particular genetic disease may be time consuming and expensive. There is no guarantee that a particular genetic disease will be caused by a single gene nor that undesirable genes won't be linked to desirable ones. Some population geneticists and a few European kennel clubs think genetic disease can be reduced quicker and more simply by discouraging close inbreeding, especially father/daughter, mother/son, and brother/sister matings.

Long, intense inbreeding within a small, closed

population can produce sterile males, reduced litter sizes, poor birthing and mothering ability. In these extreme circumstances, some population geneticists advise broadening the gene pool by outcrossing: breeding to a similar but less closely related breed.

A few European breeds have been restored to genetic health by outcrossing—and outcrossing can fix other problems as well. In the mid-seventies the AKC Wirehaired Pointing Griffon Club swallowed a bitter pill: their show-bred dogs were no longer able hunters. To regain hunting skills, they outcrossed to the Czech Fousek—a similar breed which had retained its hunting abilities.

Today the Griffon club (no longer an AKC breed club but an independent registry) breeds exclusively for hunting abilities. Should you contact the club for a pup, you'll be asked, *Are you a dedicated hunter?* If the answer to that question is no, sorry, no pup.

If you survive the initial screening, you sign a

detailed, rigorous contract and are told who has a puppy for sale (or when a litter is expected) and the price, which is set by the club (currently $650).

The club holds three realistic hunting tests of increasing complexity. Every Griffon should undergo the first two tests, and every potential sire or dam must. Someone from the club's breeding committee evaluates each young Griffon's performance. Upon the breeder's application, the breeding committee decides whether the Griffon can be bred, and if so, to which sire or dam. As one owner told me (his pup hadn't made the grade), *Deciding to neuter him was one of the hardest things I've ever done. But it was the RIGHT thing to do!* Should anyone breed without permission, the club will not register the offspring nor will it register AKC Wire-Haired Griffons.

This program has achieved its goals: the modern Wire-Haired Griffon is a versatile hunter that finds, points, flushes & retrieves upland game birds and ducks. To my eyes, the Griffon's a homely dog: something like a whiskery grey/black aire-dale. But as it works the dog becomes beautiful; handsome is as handsome does.

The AKC rarely permits outcrossing. *Makes you question what a purebred is,* Deborah Lynch, AKC Canine Health Foundation Director, told me.

• • •

Mammalian species where both parents rear their young are extremely rare: less than one percent. Humans and canids are social species; both are communicators and evolutionary opportunists—quick to fill any available ecological niche. In an evolutionary sense, we were predisposed to bond with one another. This bond is so profound that humans and dogs not infrequently sacrifice their lives for each other & simply being in the other's presence lowers blood pressure and improves cardiac health.

My wife and I work and train and walk our dogs every day in any weather, 365 days a year. Sheepdog trials are more important on my calendar than Christmas or the Fourth of July. Every evening dogs usurp our sofa and chairs; in winter months we have to step over dogs to feed the woodstove. For years my wife and I never vacationed together because who would look after the dogs?

On good days, I imagine humans are connected to our dogs on a primitive genetic level; that we don't need to hear well because our dogs hear for us, that we don't need good noses because our dogs sniff out danger, that we humans can dream because our dogs watch over us. On good days, I think dogs gave us our spiritual life.

Some skeptics say the human–dog bond—if it exists at all—is mutual neediness between an overindulgent, neurotic human and his pampered chowhound who pumps out unconditional love because it's too stupid not to. To skeptics, the doggy toys, organic dog treats, high dollar veterinary care, dog shows, dog clothing, pet cemeteries, doggy spas, and doggy beauty parlors are derisible—and perhaps even wicked: *How can you pamper a dog when children are starving in Uganda?*

And human/dog relations are often pretty ugly.

Those cherished, well-fed demining dogs I met on the Albanian border were an exception in that poor country; the mangy, garbage-scrounging stray that distracted Ellis was the rule. Many of the street dogs I saw were crippled; none wore a collar.

Some markets in Asia sell puppies as food.

The Humane Society of the United States estimates between two and three million dogs are killed every year in U.S. animal shelters.

Dogs view humans as dogs, as members of their dog pack & an awful lot of people see dogs as four-legged humans in fur coats. At the Battersea reunion one woman complained that her Pekingese bit her. Frequently. That very morning, still in bed, the little dog bit her on the stomach.

I suggested obedience training but the woman wasn't interested.

As the tiny brute growled at me, its owner

grinned approvingly: *I like someone who can say, NO!*

On bad days I think the ancient, fruitful relationship of man and dog depends on two species' mutual misunderstanding.

And yet, and yet . . . one foggy morning I bent to read the faded epitaphs in the tiny eighteenth-century dog cemetery in London's Hyde Park: MY BABA, never forgotten, never replaced. IN MEMORY of our dear old friend Smut—the first to welcome. DEAR LITTLE GOOFY—aged seven years. Sleep peacefully little one.

• • •

After twelve hours in the saddle I was glad to dismount at the bed-ground. The Helle family: Joe, Tom, John's wife Karen, and all the kids had been driving for hours on rough dirt roads, hauling the sheepherders' camps around the mountain to this new location.

All the species were happy. The weary sheep could bed down, the horses could rest, grown-ups stretched and joked while kids frolicked under that big, darkening Montana sky. The guard dogs trotted out to their posts on the outskirts of the flocks. Even John's old retired dogs, Ginger and Spike, had come here to greet their wagging offspring at the end of the trail. We rode 25 miles that day. I figure the dogs ran 150.

As John Helle said, *Without the dogs it'd be impossible.*

Uncle Harry

AFTER TWENTY years training and trialing sheep-dogs, I cannot understand why so many people assume a dog's emotional life is poorer than our own.

Harry is a powerful, short-coated, ugly, black-and-tan Border Collie. His head's so broad I've been asked if he *has any pit bull in him.* Every day Harry and I work sheep on our farm and on weekends to relax, we go to sheepdog trials. Harry's a natural dog: at a year old, before I started training, he'd sweep out in a great arc behind his sheep and bring them directly to my feet. Like most naturals, Harry resented interference and when I made

63

suggestions sometimes he'd sulk and go home. In time, he came to agree that my suggestions made things go a bit smoother but he never lost his preference for working on his own.

Harry loves the trials. When I start packing, I can't keep him out of the car. As soon as we arrive at the trial grounds he jumps out to greet all those beautiful, supple, talented, charming, albeit less than compliant bitches. When it's his turn next, he whines his pleasure.

By three years old, he'd won trials and qualified to run in the National Handler's Finals. The Handler's Finals, held that year at Lexington, Kentucky, is the World Series of sheepdog trials—Harry would run against 180 of the best sheepdogs in North America.

Harry made his natural outrun and fetch, turned his sheep around me, and set out on a horrendous drive the British judge said was the longest he'd ever seen. Near the end, Harry was losing faith but I said cheerful things to him and he finished the drive, brought them into the shedding ring, made his split, his pen, and his shed. As I walked off the course a friend came over to congratulate us and told me, *You were hyperventilating so bad in the shedding ring, I was afraid you'd pass out.* I do recall that at the time my vision was getting fuzzy at the edges, but so long as I could still see Harry and the sheep I didn't care.

Harry is our oldest male and acts as shop steward for our six Border Collies. When I scold some dog malefactor, Harry puts his heavy head on my knee and urges forbearance. Our last litter of pups was born in the deep dark winter and sometimes you have to put those pups outdoors RIGHT NOW, but our farm borders twelve thousand acres of State Game Commission land, and to a hungry bobcat, fat puppies look like breakfast. Midnight or daylight, whenever we put the puppies out into the snow Uncle Harry went along to protect them and make sure they didn't stray. Harry took to the work. Whenever a puppy started fussing in the house—be it two or three in the morning—Harry would bump open the bedroom door and jump on my chest to alert me to a puppy in distress.

Harry is my literary dog and accompanies me on book tours and readings. Harry doesn't particularly like hundreds of strangers making over him but he'll put up with it and since many people mistake Harry's natural courtesy for fondness, he gets along fine. Harry's limits are met sooner than mine: at a Baltimore NPR studio, three weeks into my last book tour, Harry went into the corner, faced away and wouldn't come out again. I did the last two weeks of the tour alone.

With Harry snoozing on the front seat beside me, we've traveled thousands of miles to dog and book events.

Harry knows how to behave, off lead, in motels, livestock markets, bookstores, tents, libraries, loading chutes, TV stations, B&B's, college classrooms, Greenwich Village, dozens of different trial fields, and once on the sixth floor of the National Geographic Society in Washington, DC.

While traveling, I take one motel bed, Harry hops up on the other. One night, in upstate New York, people in the next room had their new puppy with them and at four in the morning, Harry was pawing my chest, wondering why I wasn't letting that poor puppy outside, was I deaf or something?

Two years after his brilliant run at Lexington, Harry's runs started falling apart. He'd be his old self at home, but on the trial field he'd wallow around like he couldn't hear my whistles or, worse, he'd take matters into his own hands. I figured it was a training problem—that his old sulkiness was returning in spades. At home, on our small training field, he'd not set a paw wrong, and when we walked to the post at a trial, Harry'd look at me and say, *Of course I can do it. For goodness sake, you've seen me do it often enough.* And then Harry would wreck.

I was looking forward to the Edgeworth Trial. Good sheep, beautiful course, and, not incidentally, a trial that rewards natural dogs. It's a 650-yard outrun up a breathtakingly steep hill, and the dog is out of sight of the handler until it reaches its sheep. Four years ago, when Harry ran that course, he was beautiful and if I'd needed two commands to bring the sheep to my feet I'd not needed three.

On Saturday when Harry ran it was cool and though a light wind made the sheep spooky they weren't too bad. It takes nearly two minutes for the dog to get up that hill behind his sheep and those minutes seemed a lifetime. Harry made a perfect outrun and with my eyes shaded, I could see Harry and two sheep drifting off downhill, but three remained and I whistled Harry to stop and go back for them, but he paid me no heed and his two sheep dawdled on down the slope. Harry was with them, sure, but he had no control of them.

We retired. One of the three ewes he'd shunned had been a tough old beast and I figured Harry had opted for the two drifting off as the easier task. A sheepdog who doesn't bring all his sheep is a moral failure, sure, but every dog has his off days.

On Sunday there was no wind, cool day, terrific sheep—a chance for a fine run. Harry went out wider than before and it was easily three minutes before the sheep started to move. I whistled Harry to where he needed to be but he lagged. I yelled, *Hey!* and *Harry!* I shouted his commands. He took my commands too late or not at all, put no pressure on the sheep, and for the second day in a row they simply drifted.

I haven't been so angry at a dog in years. After we came off the field another handler said, *That dog needs an attitude adjustment.*

No, I didn't lay a hand on Harry, physical or verbal, because there's no point making a correction unless you know what you're correcting. I had run out of dog and had no idea in the world why.

I did manage to pat Harry's head before I went to bed but it was an effort.

The next day our vet told me Harry has a heart

murmur, a leaky mitral valve. That long hard out-run was too much for him. I ran out of dog because Harry ran out of heart. One might imagine Harry's emotions alone on that hill as his genes, his skills, and distant handler cried out while his oxygen-starved heart confounded his body and mind. Not me. I don't want to know.

I am grateful that in my anger, I didn't raise my hand to Harry. When things go badly and an attitude adjustment is required, it isn't always the dog who requires it.

Harry won't go to trials anymore. He'll live out his life on the farm and do simple chore work. Until I pack my bags to take some other dog to a sheepdog trial or literary event I believe he'll be happy.

Last January, Harry and I stayed with friends in Charlottesville. At midnight, when we went outside snow was falling, two or three inches, muffling the suburbs. I walked down the middle of the unmarked street while Harry ranged on both sides, over whitened lawns, underneath snow-bulked pine trees.

Some of the houses had security lights with motion sensors and wherever Harry ranged, lights blinked on. Everything ahead of us was darkness. Behind, wherever Harry had passed, it was light.

Silent Night

In December, the population of Highland County drops to twenty-five hundred. After deer season closes, the hunters go home and the summer people are long gone. In a busy day on our dirt road a dozen vehicles pass and we generally know them all. The country store in Williamsville (pop. 16) closes early.

By Thanksgiving, we like to have both freezers full, six cords of firewood undercover, and the barn full of hay. If the power goes out, we can always cook on the woodstove.

Before it gets cold, chores are muddy and clumsy but once the ground freezes hard, things get easier. We load up haywagons with ninety bales or so, haul them into the pastures, set up portable electric fences to keep the sheep off, and throw down hay morning and evening. A few inches of snow doesn't bother us. If there's a foot or more, I put chains on all four wheels of the '51 Dodge Powerwagon and feed out of that.

We're an hour and a half drive from a shopping mall and don't watch much television so we miss Santa and Rudolph and the pre-Christmas sales. Some of our neighbors decorate their mailboxes and I've seen pickup trucks with Christmas wreaths wired to the grill, but we don't bother.

Our lambing is finished in early November so by the time bad weather hits, most of the lambs are strong. We keep an eye on the weak lambs and the bummers. A bummer's mother doesn't have enough milk for him so he survives by slipping behind (unrelated) ewes while they're busy at the feed trough and nursing until the unwilling surrogate kicks him away. Bummers are easy to spot—

they feed through the wet, dirty wool in the rear so their faces are always dirty.

A couple years ago, December weather was unusually hard. It had snowed, rained on top of the snow, frozen, and another foot fell on top of that. Night temperature was below zero & it never got above ten degrees in the daytime. We have to feed heavier when it's bitter and by Christmas Eve, we'd gone through a third of our winter's hay and a full half our firewood. One sheepdog could work for an hour or two in the cold before ice packed between its toes and we swapped it for another. My wife, Anne, and I started chores at daybreak and finished at eleven, I'd put the chainsaw in the Powerwagon and cut firewood until three or so, and we'd hurry to finish evening feeding by 5:30 when it got dark.

I brought our Christmas tree home on top of a load of firewood.

Usually, we feed our best alfalfa on Christmas Eve but this year we didn't have much good hay left. Before the sun went down behind Bullpasture Mountain, it was fifteen below and the snow had a decided blue cast.

I was ready to get back indoors when Anne said three lambs weren't going to make it. They weren't trying to bum anymore, they stood outside the flock, hunched over, dirty faced and shivering. Anne said we should catch them and bring them in the house. I objected, she prevailed. They weren't hard to catch.

In a room off the kitchen we set up a four-by-four pen, bedded deeply in fresh yellow straw. We put a water bucket in one corner & hung a plastic grain feeder from the slats. We laid down a couple leaves of alfalfa.

Sheepdogs are persnickety about the proper order of things and were horrified there were lambs in the house. They went to great lengths to avoid noticing them and when they walked by the lamb pen, never gave it a sidelong glance. The lambs ate some grain, snuggled down in the straw, and didn't make a peep.

Anne likes to keep a warm house and the wood-stove was crackling. Frozen socks and coveralls dried behind the stove and the dogs sprawled around so we had to step over them.

There is an old tradition that at midnight on Christmas Eve, animals can talk and I wondered what the dogs and lambs would say to each other.

We put flashlight, shovel, coveralls, and winter boots into the back of the 4-WD Subaru, but the roads were clear all the way to Windy Cove.

Windy Cove is an old country church with stained glass windows dedicated to long dead Presbyterian preachers and a varnished parquet ceiling high overhead. It was oddly fragrant on Christmas Eve, almost springlike. There were folding chairs in the aisles.

I don't imagine many families in our congregation make more than twenty thousand dollars a year but that means we don't have much money, not that we're poor. That night, everybody wore respectful clothes and the kids' bluejeans were ironed and the older kids wore clip-on ties.

The scant accounts of the Christ child's birth in a stable have been set to music so many times, musicality is part of them, as if each phrase has background singing. *Unto us a child is born . . . It came upon a midnight clear . . .* We sang the carols that make us feel less lonely this time of year.

Our preacher, Rob Sherrard, was a navy officer before he became a preacher. He's a good preacher and sometimes inspired.

That Christmas Eve, Creigh and Pam Deeds brought their daughter to the church to be baptised.

It was cold outside the church and deep.

Before their friends & neighbors, the parents pledged to bring their daughter up in the nurture and admonition of God.

Preacher Sherrard loves and is comfortable with infants and beaming, he carried the baby into the congregation. He asked if we would act as godparents and help the parents nurture her.

We said we would.

Will you endeavor by your example and fellow-

ship to strengthen her family ties with the household of God?

We would.

The baby looked around, solemn and safe.

The preacher said, *This little girl is Amanda Deeds. Amanda's name comes from the Latin. It means, She must be loved.*

Country people who heat with wood heat are mildly paranoid and nobody lingered after the service. As we neared our farm, we were anxious to spot the lit window that meant the house was still there.

Anne crammed wood into the stove while I checked the lambs. When you stick a finger in the mouth of a healthy lamb, the mouth is warm. These lambs were fine, annoyed at being disturbed. Anne would get up at three to put wood on the fire & I'd stoke it at six.

While Anne got ready for bed, I let the dogs out to empty. It was a half moon and the tips of broomsedge poked through expanses of unmarked snow. Winter is hard for creatures we don't tend. The Milky Way splashed across the sky.

Highland County is the least populated county east of the Mississippi and though the mountains stretched for thirty miles up and down river, I couldn't see a light.

That old Christmas story just might be true. Silent Night.